BUNNOIDITY

Bunnoidity

How to be a Bunny – The Rabbit Habit

Carolyn "Bunny" Campora

Bunny Prints Books
New York, New York

ISBN 978-1-61354-000-8

Designed by Carolyn Campora
Printed in the United States of America

Bunny Prints Books
P.O. Box 2094
New York, New York 10013
www.BunnyPrintsBooks.com

For Bunny Boy

Acknowledgements

My love and gratitude go to my Mother and Father for naming me Bunny, to The Big Bunny, to Step-Mommy and everyone who has given me Bunnies, to Bunny Boy and to every Bunny I have known.

Special thanks go to those who care for Bunnies, especially to all Rabbit Rescue Societies everywhere.

This Bunny Book would not be possible without the tireless help and support of the Little Buns. Bless you.

Contents

Preface

Bunnoidity is the art of being Bunnoid, that is, Bunny-like.

Bunnies are sweet, soft and cute. Bunnies are innocent and good.

Humans respond to Bunnies with a smile, with a softening attitude, with enjoyment. In short, they respond to Bunnies by taking on Bunny-like qualities. They become gentler while feeling happier when around soft, furry Bunnies. Humans become more Bunnoid when they even think of Bunnies.

Thus, Bunnoid awareness and the practice of Bunnoidity help us to enjoy a kinder, gentler world.

Bunnoidity

How to be a Bunny – The Rabbit Habit

Chapter 1

What Is Bunnoidity

Bunnoidity is the art of being Bunnoid, that is, Bunny-like.

Chapter 2

Why Bunnoidity Is Important

Bunnies are sweet, soft, cute and, usually, little.

Bunnies are innocent and good. They want comfort and joy for themselves and others.

To be Bunnoid is to be happiness promoting. Who sees or touches a Bunny and does not smile?

When we see or touch a Bunny we feel gentler, softer and sweeter. When we feel gentler, softer and sweeter, we are nicer to others.

Humans respond to their environments. What surrounds us affects us. We are influenced by what is around us.

We naturally seek harmony. Seeking harmony in our environment, we begin to blend in with our environment, becoming more like what is around us. Seeking harmony in our environment, we begin to blend others in with our environment, perceiving them to be more like us.

If we are around Bunnies, we become more Bunnoid, that is, gentler, softer and sweeter. More Bunnoid ourselves, we now perceive others as more Bunnoid. Bunnies like other Bunnies. We like others better because we now see the Bunny in them.

When we like others better, we are nicer to them. When we are nicer to others, they are usually nicer to us. We have increased Bunnoidity in our world, and everyone is happier.

Chapter 3

Identifying Bunnoidity

Humans are innately Bunnoid when they are born and for the first few years of their lives. We smile when we look at a baby or small child. Babies and small children are little, sweet, innocent, soft and cute.

All baby animals are cute. Most animals, like humans, change quite a bit as they grow up.

Bunnies remain cute their whole lives. When Bunnies grow up they do not become less soft or less innocent. Even the biggest Bunnies just look like bigger baby Bunnies. Baby Bunnies and big Bunnies like to be around other Bunnies, eat good foodies, hop and sleep. Bunnies just don't change very much as they grow into adulthood.

By becoming more Bunnoid, we become more like little children, sweet, innocent and good.

We feel good when we look at Bunnies. When looking around for something to feel good about, just look around for something Bunnoid. There are a few pertinent questions you can ask to assess Bunnoidity.

1. Is it little? Yes? Therefore Bunnoid!

2. Is it cute? Yes? Therefore Bunnoid!

3. Is it pretty? Yes? Therefore Bunnoid!

4. Is it soft? Yes? Therefore Bunnoid!

5. Is it furry? Yes? Therefore Bunnoid!

6. Is it sweet? Yes? Therefore Bunnoid!

7. Is it gentle? Yes? Therefore Bunnoid!

8. Is it delightful? Yes? Therefore Bunnoid!

9. Is it irresistible? Yes? Therefore Bunnoid!

10. Is it fun? Yes? Therefore Bunnoid!

11. Is it bringing a smile to your face? Yes? Therefore Bunnoid!

12. Is it making you feel happy? Yes? Therefore Bunnoid!

13. Is it inspiring you to be better? Yes? Therefore Bunnoid!

Chapter 4

How Bunnies Behave – Bunnying

Bunnying is the ongoing act of being very busy, accomplishing very little, while engaging in much conversation and many instructions.

Bunnying is task oriented. It may be engaged in singly or socially. The best most Bunnoid Bunnying is done in the company of two or more Bunnies.

Bunnying may be identified through observation of Bunny behaviors.

Bunnies approach each day with an eye to maximizing enjoyment. Their sense of accomplishment may be seen as different from human standards of achievement.

Bunnies engage in Bunnying in order to enjoy the process. The product is desired, but is less important than the process.

In Bunnying, the process may extend indefinitely. As projects become long, they are completed infrequently. When projects are finished, they are over, one-time events.

However, even completed projects resulting in finished products may be extended for on-going Bunny enjoyment. Discussion after the fact is an offshoot of Bunnying that prolongs Bunnying fun. This discussion of completed Bunny projects may be repeated endlessly, like the discussions and instructions before and during the process.

Thus, Bunnying encompasses all time frames, past, present and future. Bunnying is not limited by time or space, as discussion, instruction, and the telling of Bunny Tales may occur at any distance and over any time span.

Bunnying is an art for all ages. Bunnying is an art for all projects where process is more important than product. Bunnying is fun.

14

Chapter 5

How Bunnies Relate – Bunnies with Other Bunnies

Bunnies are innately cheerful. However, they are at their happiest in the company of other Bunnies.

Bunnies would rather hang out than tussle. We can picture puppies and kittens playing together, even baby tigers. But these are predator animals. Bunnies are not aggressive by nature.

Bunnoid behavior includes sharing simple activities with family and friends. With two or more Bunnies together, conversation is bound to ensue.

Bunnying often involves doing small errands together. With conversation, errands easily turn into extended playful adventures. The shopping may get done, but the list probably grew, and some items may have been skipped. Happily, this means another trip!

16

Since Bunnying involves being very busy accomplishing very little with much discussion and many instructions and opinions, every activity begun together tends to expand. New ideas suggest new directions. Even going in circles can be fun, if done with much conversation and a relaxed attitude about goals.

Bunnies like to hop around in many directions, so road trips are a favorite. Destination, like other goals, is not as important as the trip. A Bunny Trip has a general direction and a loose schedule.

Bunnies follow their noses. And Bunny noses twitch vigorously when sensing edibles. This means snacks en route or frequent stops for foodies. Bunnies sleep when they feel like it, so reservations are less probable than unplanned stops whenever. Of course, sleep occurs only after the evening meal.

All Bunny activities shared with other Bunnies are good, therefore Bunnoid.

Chapter 6

Bunnies at Home – Importance of the Burrow

Bunnies are vulnerable and know that a protected environment is important. They love their homes. A Bunny is happy in its burrow. The burrow is a happy place when a Bunny is in it.

Bunnies have strong nesting instincts and will work to make their homes comfortable, soft and snugly.

Bunnies are not meant for deprivation. They are relaxed only when surrounded with plenty.

They need controlled temperatures. They like to be warm when it's cold and need to keep cool when it's hot. They always need an endless supply of fresh water and food.

Bunnies love to be clean. They need an environment that is healthy.

Bunnies need lots of attention and shared activity. They would rather hang out in their burrows with you than alone. They are content to nuzzle up against you and be petted.

22

Chapter 7

Ever Better Bunnies vs. UnBunnoid Behavior

Bunnies are good, therefore, being good is Bunnoid. Bad is not good, and therefore, being bad is unBunnoid. Of course, Bunnies always want to be Bunnoid, which means always exhibiting the highest and best of Bunny qualities.

Bunnies are not mean. They do not do bad things on purpose. But sometimes a Bunny may exhibit unBunnoid Behavior. What to do if you are that Bunny?

First, recognize that you are not living up to the high standards of Bunnoidity. How will you know? There are very clear signs if you are behaving in an unBunnoid way. You will know immediately if you check for these signs.

You:

1. You do not feel happy.

2. You stop smiling.

3. Your face feels tight, droopy or heavy.

4. Your ears droop.

5. You feel heavy.

6. You feel "off," not quite right.

7. Your energy drops, you feel tired.

8. Your enthusiasm drops, the "wind goes out of your sails."

9. You get an uncomfortable physical sense, like tension or a knot in your stomach.

10. You feel guilty.

11. You wonder if you have been bad. Ask yourself "Have I been bad?" or "Was I bad?"

Around you:

1. Someone stops smiling.

2. Their face looks tight, droopy or heavy.

3. They seem to shrink, sag or droop.

4. They lose energy and act tired.

5. They get sad.

6. They get mad.

7. They turn away.

Bunnies are brave. Bunnies readily admit the truth because they always want to be better.

The better a Bunny is, the less tolerable unBunnoid behavior is.

Bunnies know that happiness lies in making others happy. They know that the surest way to make others happy is by being good, loveable and sweet.

Remember, bad is not good, and Bunnies are good. Therefore, being bad is unBunnoid, being good is Bunnoid.

And a Bunny can always be an Ever Better Bunny.

Chapter 8

Bunnoidity for a Better World

Bunnoidity makes for happiness.

Happiness makes for positive interactions. Positive interactions make for peace. Peace makes for prosperity. Prosperity makes for contentment. Contentment makes for Bunnying.

To Bunny is to relax and enjoy the moment.

To be Bunnoid is to be loveable, sweet and good.

To be sweet and good is to inspire others to be sweet and good.

With more sweetness and goodness, everyone is happier, and the world is a better place.

Let us Bunny and be Bunnoid. Here's to Bunnoidity!

There's Always Room

For More Bunnies

About the Author

Carolyn "Bunny" Campora was called
Bunny from the moment she was born.
Family and friends continue to call her
Bunny. True, as a wellness professional she
is known as Carolyn, and in her Tai Chi
and Kung Fu classes as Master Carolyn or

Master Campora. Still, her best friend, "Dr. Nan," gave her a t-shirt that says "Master Bun." And everyone welcomes the light-spirited inclusion of ridiculousness as an effective ingredient in the pursuit of self development at Nabi Su Martial Arts & Wellness Center.

Bunny Campora has explored examples and nuances of Bunnoidity throughout her life. Her increasing appreciation of the need of the world for more Bunnoidity has inspired her to bring forth this philosophy for all to enjoy.

Education, Influences: Davis Elementary, Dominican Convent Upper School, University of California Santa Cruz, New York Studio School of Drawing, Painting & Sculpture, Cornell University Johnson Graduate School of Management, Yun Mu Kwan Karate and Nabi Su Martial Arts, Ibiki Ken Reiki, Resonance Repatterning Institute, travel, opera, family, friends and Bunnies everywhere.

www.BunnyPrintsBooks.com

www.NabiSu.com

www.ingramcontent.com/pod-product-compliance
Lightning Source LLC
Chambersburg PA
CBHW040034110426
42741CB00030B/23